The People behind the

Thomas Hunter II, Author

Thomas previously worked as a Developer Architect of a large file-sharing and storage service, where his main concern was getting a well-documented API into the hands of third-party developers. While working at a company in the financial industry he evangelized an internal API façade to abstract backend disparity. He's also given various talks on the topic of API Design. His previous book Backbone.js Application Development guides the reader through the process of building an API-consuming JavaScript application.

John Sheehan, Technical Reviewer

John is an API fanatic with over 15 years of experience working in a wide variety of IT and software development roles. As an early employee at Twilio, John lead the developer evangelism program and worked as a Product Manager for Developer Experience. After Twilio, John was Platform Lead at IFTTT working with API providers to create new channels. John is also the creator of RestSharp, API Digest, API Jobs and co-host of Traffic and Weather, an API and cloud podcast.

Jon Kuperman, Influence

I'd like to make a special thanks to Jon, who once told me "Tom, you should turn that API blog post into a book."

Introduction

An API represents a contract between the data and business-logic stored on your Server, and Consumers who wish to interact with this data. Breaking this contract will result in angry emails from developers and anguished users with broken apps. Designing a hard-to-use API will result in few or no third-party developers using it. On the other hand, building a great API and adhering to this contract will result in substantially more third-party developers and can elevate your service from a closed-source product to an open platform.

Building an API is one of the most important things you can do to increase the value of your service. By having an API, your service/application has the potential to become a platform from which other services grow. Look at these tech companies offering popular services: Facebook, Twitter, Google, GitHub, Amazon, Netflix, Dropbox... None of them would be nearly as popular as they are today if they hadn't opened their data and functionality via API. An entire industry exists with the sole purpose of consuming data provided by these platforms (Facebook games, social-media CRMs, secure Dropbox tools...)

The principles of this book, if followed while designing and maintaining an API, will ensure third-party developers grok your API while consequently reducing support tickets and emails. Developers will travel from tech conference to tech conference rejoicing what a pleasure working with your API has been, getting more developers to sign-up along the way.

Approach

This book will take a language-agnostic approach to demonstrating good API design. While there will be a few code examples here and there, you won't actually need to run any of them to understand what is happening. In fact, many of the topics are more philosophical than technical, and this book will make a great candidate for sitting on the back of your toilet.

Intended Audience

The ideal reader of this book is someone who has already built several websites and is comfortable working with a web language or framework, as well as having some intermediate knowledge such as how to read and write HTTP headers.

While knowledge of any particular language is not a requirement of this book, a basic understanding of SQL will be beneficial for understanding the example queries.

Goals

By the time you're done reading this book you'll have a high-level understanding of how to build an HTTP API Ecosystem which third-party developers will love. This book will not cover the technical details of how to program an API from scratch.

Contents

1 The Basics   **7**
  1.1 Data Design and Abstraction 7
      1.1.1 Examples of Abstraction 8
      1.1.2 Real World Examples 10
  1.2 Anatomy of an HTTP Message 11
      1.2.1 HTTP Request 12
      1.2.2 HTTP Response 12
      1.2.3 Debugging HTTP Traffic 13
  1.3 API Entrypoint 13
      1.3.1 Choosing an Entrypoint 14
      1.3.2 Content Located at the Root 15

2 API Requests   **17**
  2.1 HTTP Methods 17
  2.2 URL Endpoints 19
      2.2.1 Top-Level Collections 20
      2.2.2 Specific Endpoints 20
  2.3 Filtering Resources 22
  2.4 White-Listing Attributes 23
      2.4.1 Filtered Request 24
      2.4.2 Unfiltered Request 24
  2.5 Body Formats 25
      2.5.1 JSON 25
      2.5.2 Form URL Encoded 25
      2.5.3 Multi-Part Form Data 26

3 API Responses   **27**
  3.1 HTTP Status Codes 27
      3.1.1 Common API Status Codes 27
      3.1.2 Status Code Ranges 28
  3.2 Content Types 29
  3.3 Expected Body Content 30
  3.4 JSON Attribute Conventions 32
      3.4.1 Consistency between Resources 32
      3.4.2 Booleans 33
      3.4.3 Timestamps 33

	3.4.4	Resource Identifiers (IDs)	35
	3.4.5	Nulls	35
	3.4.6	Arrays	35
	3.4.7	Whitespace	35
3.5	Error Reporting		36
	3.5.1	Validation Errors	36
	3.5.2	Generic Errors	37
	3.5.3	Always Handle Server Errors	37
	3.5.4	String-Based Error Codes	38
3.6	Responses should Mimic Requests		39
	3.6.1	Acceptable Discrepancy	39
	3.6.2	Avoidable Discrepancy	40

4 The API Ecosystem   41

4.1	API Versioning		41
	4.1.1	Requesting a Specific Version	42
4.2	Authentication and Authorization		43
	4.2.1	Two-Legged Authentication (2LA)	43
	4.2.2	Three-Legged Authentication (3LA)	46
	4.2.3	Real-World Usage	47
4.3	Consumer Permissions		48
	4.3.1	Per-Authorization Permissions	49
	4.3.2	Default Consumer Permissions	50
4.4	Rate Limiting		51
4.5	API Analytics		51
4.6	Documentation		52
4.7	Convenience of Developer Testing		53
	4.7.1	Web-Based Developer Console	53
	4.7.2	Providing cURL Commands	54

5 HTTP API Standards   57

5.1	Hypermedia API's		57
	5.1.1	ATOM: An Early Hypermedia API	58
5.2	Response Document Standards		59
	5.2.1	JSON Schema	60
	5.2.2	JSON API	60
	5.2.3	Siren	61
5.3	Alternatives to URL-based API's		63
	5.3.1	JSON RPC	63
	5.3.2	SOAP	64

Chapter 1

The Basics

1.1 Data Design and Abstraction

Designing a friendly HTTP API means abstracting the intricate business-logic and data your service uses into the four basic CRUD concepts (*Create*, *Read*, *Update*, *Delete*). Your application may perform many complex actions behind the scenes such as sending a text message or resizing an image or moving a file, but if you do enough planning and abstraction, everything can be represented as CRUD.

Architecting your API begins earlier than you may think; first you need to decide how your data will be stored and how your service/application functions. If you're practicing API-First Development [1] this is all part of the process. However, if you're bolting an API onto an existing project, you will have more abstraction to take care of.

In an idealized, overly-simple service, a Collection can represent a database table, and a Resource can represent a row within that table. As real-world practice will show this is rarely the case, especially if the existing data design is overly complex. It is important that you don't overwhelm third-party developers with complex application data, otherwise they won't want to use your API.

There will be parts of your service which you *should not* expose via API at all. A common example is that many APIs will not allow Consumers to create or delete user accounts, or data shared between many accounts.

Sometimes multiple tables will be represented as a single resource (`JOIN` statements come in handy here). You might even find that one table should have multiple resources (although, you may have made some poor database design decisions if this is the case).

1.1.1 Examples of Abstraction

For both of these examples of abstraction, we'll make use of the same fictional service. This service sends messages to different users, and messages can either be sent as a text message or an email. The chosen method depends on the preference of the particular user.

Don't worry too much about the technical parts of the examples as we'll cover them with more detail in a later chapter. For now, just think of them as simple function calls with inputs and outputs.

1.1.1.1 Good Abstraction

Here's a clean and simple approach for sending a notification.

Creating a Notification

```
POST /notifications

{
  "user_id": "12",
  "message": "Hello World"
}

{
  "id": "1000",
  "user_id": "12",
  "message": "Hello World",
  "medium": "email",
  "created": "2013-01-06T21:02:00Z"
}
```

In this example we use a single endpoint for sending a notification to a user. The first JSON document is the request and the second is the response. This endpoint is called **notifications**, and the Consumer interacts by creating new notification objects. When the Consumer wishes to notify a user, it is conceptually creating a new notification object, thereby abstracting the concept of performing an action with creating an object.

An important concept of this example is that the business-logic of determining which method of contacting a user is abstracted

1.1. DATA DESIGN AND ABSTRACTION

away from the Consumer entirely, hence the lack of an endpoint for getting the users notification preference. In the background, the Server is taking the appropriate action and hiding it from the Consumer.

In the example response, we do have a `medium` attribute which represents the method of notifying the user, but that can be omitted depending on if your Consumers need to know this information (perhaps their application has a dashboard which mentions the last time a text/email was sent, and the verbiage should be correct).

1.1.1.2 Bad Abstraction

This example will include numerous shortcomings, and is an easy approach to take by the novice HTTP API architect.

Getting User Preference

```
GET /get_user_preferences/12

{
  "notification_preference": 1
}
```

This first API Endpoint is called `get_user_preferences`, and is called by passing in the ID of the user whose preference we are looking up (shown here as 12). The name of an Endpoint should be a simple noun (or compound nouns). It should not include the action (verb) being performed (in this case `get`). The reason one should use a simple noun is because this removes ambiguity and tells the Consumer what the ID represents. Does the 12 represent user 12? Or perhaps some user-preference concept which might not correlate 1:1 to a user object?

Another problem with this example is the response contains the integer 1. Internally to this fictional service there are some constants where 1 refers to sending a text, and 2 refers to sending an email. Even if these values are disclosed in the API documentation, a third-party developer is not going to remember what they represent. Each time they look up what the values mean they are losing productivity.

Yet another problem is that there's an API Endpoint dedicated specifically to getting a user preference. In general, you want to reduce the number of Endpoints in your API, and focus on making each one serve the Consumer better. Data like this could have been merged with another endpoint for getting a user object, for example.

Sending a Text or Email (Two Endpoints)

POST /users/12/send_{medium}

```
{
  "message": "Hello World",
  "sent": "2013-01-06T21:02:00Z"
}
```

These second and third endpoints (assuming {medium} can represent email or text) have the same problem as the previous endpoint wherein the action is part of the URL (in this case send). These endpoints don't represent data, as the previous one did, they specifically represent an action. Building APIs with these actionable endpoints is a common mistake among developers intending to build an HTTP API.

Another issue with this example is that the business-logic for determining which method of notification to use is left for the Consumer to decide! Sure, the Consumer can make a request to get the users preference, but what if they intentionally ignore it? Or suppose the Consumer caches the preference and it becomes outdated? Either way users are bound to get notified in a manner they didn't choose.

Whenever you find yourself creating two endpoints with the same request inputs and response outputs, there may be a problem with abstraction and the two may be better off combined into one endpoint.

Finally, there is no way to look up previous instances of notifications that have been sent to a user. While another Endpoint could have been created for looking up notification logs, it would likely be ad-hoc or inconsistent with existing Endpoints.

1.1.2 Real World Examples

Let's look at some real-world examples of how popular APIs do their data abstraction.

1.1.2.1 GitHub: An Ideal Example

The current GitHub v3 API [2] is a beautiful example of a properly-abstracted HTTP API. Each of the popular HTTP verbs are used where applicable. Endpoints don't have verbs in the name. Interacting with an endpoint feels much like one is working with a representation of an object, instead of performing actions.

An example of a good endpoint is `GET /repos/{user_id}/{repo_id}/notifications`. This is obviously the endpoint used for getting a list of notifications of a particular repository. The `{user_id}/{repo_id}` convention for referring to a repository is one understood by most users of GitHub (repository names aren't globally unique, only unique to a particular user). The only thing that could be improved may be to not shorten `repositories` to `repos` and `organizations` to `orgs` in the names of endpoints, although `repo` is well understood.

1.1.2.2 Twitter: A Flawed Example

The current Twitter v1.1 API [3] has some abstraction shortcomings with their data and business-logic, as far as being an HTTP API is concerned. The API only makes use of the GET and POST methods for interacting with data. Due to this shortcoming, most endpoint names are a pair of noun and verbs.

One such example is `POST /statuses/destroy/{status_id}`, used for deleting a status. A cleaner version of this endpoint would be `DELETE /statuses/{status_id}`. Also worth noting is the differentiation of `POST /statuses/update_with_media` and `POST /statuses/update`. Both of these endpoints are used for creating a new tweet, however the prior allows for the attachment of media. These two endpoints should be combined into a single `POST /statuses`, with the media related attributes being optional.

These endpoints are also an example of a bad nomenclature. Users of Twitter don't think of using the service as *updating their status*, they think of it as *tweeting*. This is something that may have changed throughout the lifetime of the service, and if so would be a good candidate to change between API versions. The Collection used by the aforementioned Endpoints would therefor be better named `tweets`.

1.2 Anatomy of an HTTP Message

Since HTTP is the protocol we're using to build our API, let's examine some raw HTTP messages. It's surprising how many developers who have been building websites for years don't know what an HTTP message looks like! When the Consumer sends a request to the Server, it provides a Request-Line and a set of Key/Value pairs called headers. For POST, PUT, and PATCH requests it also provides two newlines and then the the request body. All This information is sent in the same HTTP request (although this request can be broken up into multiple network packets if the message is large enough).

The Server then replies in a similar format, first with a Status-Line and headers, and typically two newlines followed by a body (the body is technically optional, as you'll find out later). HTTP is very much a request/response protocol; there is no *push* support (the Server does not send data to the Consumer unprovoked). To do that you would need to use a different protocol such as Websockets.

1.2.1 HTTP Request

```
POST /v1/animal HTTP/1.1
Host: api.example.org
Accept: application/json
Content-Type: application/json
Content-Length: 24

{
  "name": "Gir",
  "animal_type": "12"
}
```

1.2.2 HTTP Response

```
HTTP/1.1 200 OK
Date: Wed, 18 Dec 2013 06:08:22 GMT
Content-Type: application/json
Access-Control-Max-Age: 1728000
Cache-Control: no-cache

{
  "id": "12",
  "created": "2013-12-18T06:08:22Z",
  "modified": null,
  "name": "Gir",
  "animal_type": "12"
}
```

1.2.3 Debugging HTTP Traffic

Postman (a Google Chrome extension) is an excellent tool for interacting with an HTTP API. As seen in Figure 1.1, Postman provides a powerful yet easy-to-use interface for building API requests, as well as debugging the content of API responses. It also provides many advanced features regarding authentication (which we'll cover in later chapters).

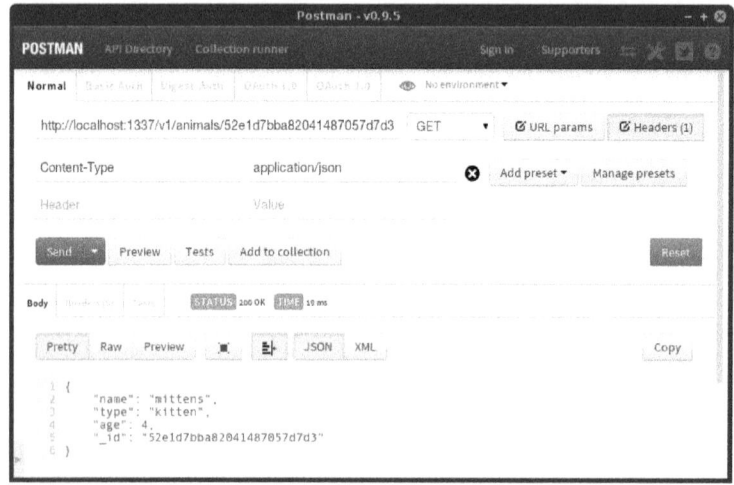

Figure 1.1: Postman Screenshot

While designing and debugging your API you will sometimes need to debug packets at a lower level than HTTP. A powerful tool for doing this is Wireshark. You will also want to use a web framework and server which allows you to read and change as many headers as possible.

Figure 1.2 is an example of a complex HTTP request from a form submission on a website. Notice all of the data sent back and forth via HTTP headers. The headers passed around by browsers and web servers is often more chaotic and noisy than what an API Consumer and Server will send.

1.3 API Entrypoint

The root location of your API is important, believe it or not. When a third-party developer (aka *code archaeologist*) inherits a project

Figure 1.2: Wireshark Screenshot

using your API and needs to build new features, they may not know about your service at all. Perhaps all they know is a list of URLs which the Consumer communicates with. It's important that the root entry point into your API is as simple as possible, as a long complex URL will appear daunting and can turn developers away.

1.3.1 Choosing an Entrypoint

Here are two common URL schemes that developers use when building an API. These are also sometimes called API entry points.

- https://api.example.com/* – *Preferred*
- https://example.org/api/* – *Security Implications*

First, notice the HTTPS prefix. If API communication is sent unencrypted over the Internet, any third-party along the way is able to eavesdrop. This could include reading sensitive API data, and depending on the chosen authentication method, could allow third-parties to make requests on behalf of the user.

If your application is huge, or you anticipate it becoming huge, putting the API on a dedicated subdomain (in this case api.) is a

1.3. API ENTRYPOINT

must. This will allow for more scalability options in the future. It can also be useful for controlling what cookie data can be shared between the content website and the API.

If you anticipate your API will never become large, or you want to build a simple application (e.g. you want to host the website AND API from the same framework), or if your API is entirely anonymous or read-only, placing your API beneath a URL segment at the root of the domain (e.g. `/api/`) will also work, however it is not a great idea. More considerations will need to be made regarding security, and more potential vulnerabilities can arise. For example, if an XSS vulnerability is discovered on the main website, credentials which might not otherwise be exposed can now be hijacked by a devious third-party.

Do not use a different Top Level Domain (TLD) for hosting your API than for hosting your website. This may sound tempting, as your main domain could be **example.com**, and your API and developer documentation be entirely located on the trendy **example.io**. However there is no logical relationship between these two domains as an adversary could have purchased **example.io**, posing as a legitimate counterpart to **example.com**. Also, the *code archaeologist* might only have knowledge of one domain and not the other. Finally, if you *do* want to share cookies between the two domains (e.g. an authenticated user on **example.com** can be automatically logged into the developer site) it cannot be done as easily with two separate TLDs than with a subdomain or even a subdirectory.

1.3.2 Content Located at the Root

It's beneficial to Consumers to have content at the root of your API. For example, accessing the root of GitHub's API returns a listing of endpoints. Personally I'm a fan of having the root URL give information which a lost developer would find useful, like how to get to the developer documentation.

Here's a truncated list of the content provided by the GitHub API Entrypoint.

```
{
  "current_user_url": "https://api.github.com/user",
  "authorizations_url":
    "https://api.github.com/authorizations",
  "emails_url": "https://api.github.com/user/emails",
  "starred_url":
```

```
    "https://api.github.com/user/starred{/owner}{/repo}",
    ...
}
```

The syntax used to describe these URLs is called a URI Template and is a human-readable and machine-parsable standard for describing URLs. This is a great way to convey URLs in both your API documentation, as well as the API responses themselves.

> A URI Template is a compact sequence of characters for describing a range of Uniform Resource Identifiers through variable expansion. [4]

Information about the currently-authenticated user can also be placed in the root of the API. As an example, either the user ID or URL to the user would make a great candidate. If you take a similar approach to what GitHub does, one of the keys could be current_user, and the value could be a URL to the users endpoint pre-populated with the current users user_id.

It may be tempting to create an endpoint called /user or /users/me for accessing information about the current user, but these would contradict the existing URL patterns the rest of the API adheres to.

Chapter 2

API Requests

2.1 HTTP Methods

You probably already know about GET and POST requests. These are the two most commonly used requests when a web browser accesses webpages and interacts with data. All browsers, including the antiquated Internet Explorer 6 (IE6), are able to generate these two requests.

There are, however, four and a half HTTP Methods that you need to know about when building an HTTP API. I say *and a half* because the PATCH method is very similar to the PUT method, and the functionality of the two are often combined into just PUT by many APIs.

You've likely heard of the phrase *CRUD* when referring to the seemingly boiler-plate code many web developers need to write when interacting with a database. Some web frameworks will even generate CRUD *Scaffolding* for the developer as a result of running a simple terminal command. CRUD stands for Create, Read, Update, and Delete, and short of handling any business-logic, can be used for handling all data entry.

Here is a list of HTTP Methods, as well as which CRUD operation they represent, and if your service were to represent an extremely simple database, the associated SQL command.

- **GET** (Read)
    - Retrieve a specific Resource from the Server
    - Retrieve a Collection of Resources from the Server

- Considered *Safe*: this request should not alter server state
- Considered *Idempotent*: duplicate subsequent requests should be side-effect free
- Corresponds to a SQL SELECT command

- **POST** (Create)
    - Creates a new Resource on the Server
    - Corresponds to a SQL INSERT command

- **PUT** (Update)
    - Updates a Resource on the Server
    - Provide the entire Resource
    - Considered *Idempotent*: duplicate subsequent requests should be side-effect free
    - Corresponds to a SQL UPDATE command, providing null values for missing columns

- **PATCH** (Update)
    - Updates a Resource on the Server
    - Provide only changed attributes
    - Corresponds to a SQL UPDATE command, specifying only columns being updated

- **DELETE** (Delete)
    - Destroys a Resource on the Server
    - Considered *Idempotent*: duplicate subsequent requests should be side-effect free
    - Corresponds to a SQL DELETE command

Here are two lesser-known HTTP Methods. While it isn't always necessary that they be implemented in your API, in some situations (such as API's accessed via web browser from a different domain), their inclusion is mandatory.

- **HEAD**
    - Retrieve metadata about a Resource (just the headers)

                – E.g. a hash of the data or when it was last updated
                – Considered *Safe*: this request should not alter server state
                – Considered *Idempotent*: duplicate subsequent requests should be side-effect free

        - **OPTIONS**
                – Retrieve information about what the Consumer can do with the Resource
                – Modern browsers precede all CORS requests with an OPTIONS request
                – Considered *Safe*: this request should not alter server state
                – Considered *Idempotent*: duplicate subsequent requests should be side-effect free

By making use of the HTTP methods, and not using actionable-verbs within the URL itself, a simpler interface is presented to the developer. Instead of wondering which verbs apply to which nouns (Do I `send` or `mail` an *email*? Do I `remove` or `fire` an *employee*?), a unambiguous and consistent convention is provided instead.

Typically, GET requests can be cached (and often are!) Browsers, for example, will cache GET requests (depending on expiration headers), and will go as far as alert the user if they attempt to POST data for a second time. A HEAD request is basically a GET without the response body, and can be cached as well.

If you plan on allowing JavaScript Consumers running within web browsers, and making requests from different domains, the OPTIONS method will need to be supported. There is a fairly-new concept called Cross Origin Resource Sharing (CORS) which uses the OPTIONS header. Basically, it provides a set of request and response headers for defining which domains can access data and which HTTP Methods they can utilize.

2.2 URL Endpoints

An Endpoint is a URL within your API which provides a method to interact with a Resource or a Collection of Resources. A typical HTTP API will use a plural naming convention for Collections.

2.2.1 Top-Level Collections

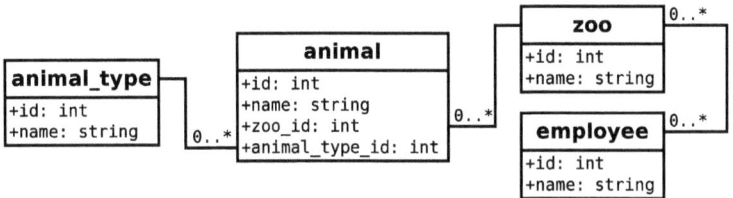

Figure 2.1: Diagram of Relationships

If you were building a fictional API to represent several different Zoo's, each containing many Animals (with an animal belonging to exactly one Zoo), employees (who can work at multiple Zoos) and keeping track of the species of each animal, you might have the following endpoints:

- `https://api.example.com/v1/zoos`
- `https://api.example.com/v1/animals`
- `https://api.example.com/v1/animal_types`
- `https://api.example.com/v1/employees`

Each piece of data separated by a slash is a URL Segment. Try to keep the number of segments per endpoint as few as possible.

2.2.2 Specific Endpoints

While conveying what each endpoint does, you'll want to list valid HTTP Method and Endpoint combinations. For example, here's a list of actions one can perform with our fictional Zoo-keeping API. Notice that we precede each endpoint with the HTTP Method. This is a common notation and is similar to the one used within an HTTP Request header.

- `GET /v1/zoos`: List all Zoos (perhaps just ID and Name, not too much detail)
- `POST /v1/zoos`: Create a new Zoo
- `GET /v1/zoos/{zoo_id}`: Retrieve an entire Zoo resource
- `PUT /v1/zoos/{zoo_id}`: Update a Zoo (entire resource)

2.2. URL ENDPOINTS

- PATCH /v1/zoos/{zoo_id}: Update a Zoo (partial resource)
- DELETE /v1/zoos/{zoo_id}: Delete a Zoo
- GET /v1/zoos/{zoo_id}/animals: Retrieve a listing of Animals (ID and Name)
- GET /v1/animals: List all Animals (ID and Name)
- POST /v1/animals: Create a new Animal
- GET /v1/animals/{animal_id}: Retrieve an Animal resource
- PUT /v1/animals/{animal_id}: Update an Animal (entire resource)
- PATCH /v1/animals/{animal_id}: Update an Animal (partial resource)
- GET /v1/animal_types: Retrieve a listing (ID and Name) of all Animal Types
- GET /v1/animal_types/{animaltype_id}: Retrieve an entire Animal Type resource
- GET /v1/employees: Retrieve an entire list of Employees
- GET /v1/employees/{employee_id}: Retrieve a specific Employee
- GET /v1/zoos/{zoo_id}/employees: Retrieve a listing of Employees at this Zoo
- POST /v1/employees: Create a new Employee
- POST /v1/zoos/{zoo_id}/employees: Hire an Employee at a specific Zoo
- DELETE /v1/zoos/{zoo_id}/employees/{employee_id}: Fire an Employee from a Zoo

The Entrypoint prefix has been omitted in the above examples for brevity. While this can be fine during informal communication (or books with limited page width), in your actual API documentation you should display the full URL to each endpoint.

Notice how the relationships between data is conveyed, for example the many-to-many relationships between Employees and Zoos.

By adding an additional URL segment, one can perform relationship interactions. Of course there is no HTTP verb for "FIRE"-ing an employee, but by performing a DELETE on an Employee located within a Zoo, we're able to achieve the same goal.

Also notice how the listing of Endpoints doesn't include every possible method-to-resource combination. For example a Consumer is unable to POST or DELETE to the `animal_types` Endpoints. In this fictional situation, only administrators would be able to add new `animal_types` using some mechanism outside of the API.

There's nothing wrong with not supporting every method-to-resource combination, as every conceptual data manipulation your service offers doesn't necessarily need to be exposed via API. Just keep in mind developers may wonder why certain features aren't available, and they may even attempt to use an undocumented Endpoint (such as DELETE-ing an `animal_type`). Know that if the functionality isn't documented, a developer may still discover a hidden feature by brute force.

2.3 Filtering Resources

When a Consumer makes a GET request for a Collection, provide them a list of every Resource matching the requested criteria, even though the list could be quite large. Do your best to minimize arbitrary limitations imposed on Consumers, as these limits make it harder for a third party developer to grok the API. If they request a Collection, and iterate over the results, never seeing more than 100 items, it is now their mission to determine where this limit is imposed. Is their ORM buggy and limiting items to 100? Is the network chopping up large responses?

Do offer the ability for a Consumer to specify some sort of filtering/limitation of the results. The most important reason for this, as far as the Consumer is concerned, is that the network payload is minimal and the Consumer receives results as soon as possible. Another reason for this is the Consumer may be lazy and want the Server to perform filtering and pagination. The not-so-important reason from the Consumers perspective, yet a great benefit for the Server, is that response-generation will require less resources.

Since these are GET requests on Collections, filters should be passed via URL parameters. Here are some examples of the types of filtering you could conceivably add to your API, and if your API were a simple representation of a Relational Database, the correlating SQL clause.

- `?limit=10&offset=20`: Pagination and offsetting of results
  (`LIMIT 20, 10`)

- `?animal_type_id=1`: Filter records which match the following condition
  (`WHERE animal_type_id = 1`)

- `?sort_attribute=name,asc`: Sort the results based on the specified attributes
  (`ORDER BY name ASC`)

Some filtering can be redundant with other endpoints. In the Endpoints section we had a `GET /zoo/{zoo_id}/animals` Endpoint. This would be the same thing as `GET /animals?zoo_id={zoo_id}`. Dedicated endpoints will make API consumption easier for developers. This is especially true with requests you anticipate will be made frequently. In the documentation, mention this redundancy so that developers aren't left wondering what the differences is.

2.4 White-Listing Attributes

Often times, when a Consumer is making a GET request to a specific Resource or Collection, they do not need all attributes belonging to the resource(s). Having so much data could become a network bottleneck as well. Responding with less data can help reduce server overhead, e.g. it may prevent an unnecessary database JOIN.

Again, since we're dealing with GET requests, you'll want to accept a URL parameter for white-listing attributes. In theory, black-listing could work as well, but as new attributes appear in Resources (since additions are backwards compatible), the Consumer ends up receiving data it doesn't want.

The parameter name you choose isn't too important. It could be `filter` or the overly-verbose `attribute_whitelist`. Consistency between different Endpoints is what is most important.

The SQL queries in these examples are over-simplification of what could be generated if your API represented a simple Relational Database application.

2.4.1 Filtered Request

In this example, the Consumer has requested a filtered list of attributes pertaining to a user.

Request URL

GET http://api.example.org/user/12?whitelist=id,name,email

Resulting SQL Query

SELECT id, name, email FROM user WHERE user.id = 12;

Response Body

```
{
  "id": "12",
  "name": "Thomas Hunter II",
  "email": "me@thomashunter.name"
}
```

2.4.2 Unfiltered Request

In this example request, the default representation of a user resource includes data from two database tables joined together. One of the tables is a **user** table, and another table contains some textual data related to a user called **user_desc**.

Request URL

GET http://api.example.org/user/12

Resulting SQL Query

SELECT * FROM user LEFT JOIN user_desc ON
    user.id = user_desc.id WHERE user.id = 12;

Response Body

```
{
  "id": "12",
  "name": "Thomas Hunter II",
  "age": 27,
  "email": "me@thomashunter.name",
  "description": "Blah blah blah blah blah."
}
```

2.5 Body Formats

A common method for APIs to receive data from third-parties is to accept a JSON document as the body. Assuming your API provides data to third-parties in the form of JSON, as a consequence those same third-parties should also be able to produce JSON documents.

There are two primary methods a Web Browser will use when sending data to a web server. If you're using a popular web language/framework for building an API, such as *PHP* or *Express.js* and *Ruby on Rails*, you're already used to consuming data using these two methods. Web Servers (e.g. *Apache* or *NGINX*) abstract the differences of these two methods and will provide your programming language one easy method to consume data. The two methods are called Multi-part Form Data (required for file uploads), and URL Form Encoded (most forms use this latter method).

2.5.1 JSON

The JSON document used for the Request can be very similar to the JSON document used for the Response. JSON can specify the type of data (e.g. Integers, Strings, Booleans), while also allowing for hierarchal relationships of data. String data needs to be escaped (e.g. a quote " becomes prefixed with a backslash \"), but this is typically done automatically for the developer.

```
POST /v1/animal HTTP/1.1
Host: api.example.org
Accept: application/json
Content-Type: application/json
Content-Length: 24

{
  "name": "Gir",
  "animal_type": "12"
}
```

2.5.2 Form URL Encoded

This method is used by Websites for accepting simple data forms from a web browser. Data needs to be URL Encoded if it contains any special characters (e.g. a space character becomes %20). This is automatically taken care of by the browser.

```
POST /login HTTP/1.1
```

```
Host: example.com
Content-Length: 31
Accept: text/html
Content-Type: application/x-www-form-urlencoded

username=root&password=Zion0101
```

2.5.3 Multi-Part Form Data

This method is used by Websites for accepting more complex data from a web browser, such as file uploads. No escaping needs to happen, although the boundary is a random string and needs to not be contained within the uploaded file or form data.

```
POST /file_upload HTTP/1.1
Host: example.com
Content-Length: 275
Accept: text/html
Content-Type: multipart/form-data; boundary=----RANDOM_jDMUxq

------RANDOM_jDMUxq
Content-Disposition: form-data; name="file"; filename="h.txt"
Content-Type: application/octet-stream

Hello World
------RANDOM_jDMUxq
Content-Disposition: form-data; name="some_checkbox"

on
------RANDOM_jDMUxq--
```

Chapter 3

API Responses

3.1 HTTP Status Codes

It is vital that an HTTP API makes use of the proper HTTP Status Codes; they are a standard after all! Various networking equipment is able to read these Status Codes, e.g. load balancers can be configured to avoid sending requests to a web server sending out too many errors. Client libraries understand if a request has succeeded or failed depending on the Status Code.

> The first line of a Response message is the Status-Line, consisting of the protocol version followed by a numeric status code and its associated textual phrase, with each element separated by SP characters. No CR or LF is allowed except in the final CRLF sequence. [5]

Here is an example of what a complete Status-Line looks like:

`HTTP/1.1 404 File Not Found`

3.1.1 Common API Status Codes

While there are a plethora of HTTP Status Codes to choose from [5], this list should provide a good starting point.

- 200 OK
    - Successful GET / PUT / PATCH Requests
    - The Consumer requested data from the Server, and the Server found it for them

– The Consumer gave the Server data, and the Server accepted it

- 201 `Created`

    – Successful POST Requests
    – The Consumer gave the Server data, and the Server accepted it

- 204 `No Content`

    – Successful DELETE Requests
    – The Consumer asked the Server to delete a Resource, and the Server deleted it

- 400 `Invalid Request`

    – Erroneous POST / PUT / PATCH Requests
    – The Consumer gave bad data to the Server, and the Server did nothing with it

- 404 `Not Found`

    – All Requests
    – The Consumer referenced an inexistent Resource or Collection

- 500 `Internal Server Error`

    – All Requests
    – The Server encountered an error, and the Consumer does not know if the request succeeded

3.1.2 Status Code Ranges

The first digit of the status code is the most significant, and provides a generalization of what the entire code is for.

3.1.2.1 1XX - Informational

The **1XX** range is reserved for low-level HTTP happenings, and you'll very likely go your entire career without manually sending one of these status codes. An example of this range is when upgrading a connection from HTTP to Web Sockets.

3.1.2.2 2XX - Successful

The **2XX** range is reserved for successful responses. Ensure your Server sends as many of these to the Consumer as possible.

3.1.2.3 3XX - Redirection

The **3XX** range is reserved for traffic redirection triggering subsequent requests. Most APIs do not use these status codes however the newer Hypermedia style APIs may make more use of them.

3.1.2.4 4XX - Client Error

The **4XX** range is reserved for responding to errors made by the Consumer, e.g. they've provided bad data or asked for something which don't exist. These requests should be be idempotent, and not change the state of the server.

3.1.2.5 5XX - Server Error

The **5XX** range is reserved as a response when the Server makes a mistake. Often times, these errors are created by low-level functions even outside of the developers control to ensure a Consumer gets some sort of response. The Consumer can't possibly know the state of the server when a **5XX** response is received, e.g. did a failure happen before or after persisting the change, and so these should be avoidable.

3.2 Content Types

Currently, the most *exciting* of APIs provide JSON data via HTTP. This includes Facebook, Twitter, GitHub, etc. XML appears to have lost the popularity contest a while ago (save for large corporate environments). SOAP, thankfully, is all but dead. We really don't see many APIs providing HTML to be consumed (except for web scrapers).

Figure 3.1 is a Google Trends graph comparing the terms *JSON API*, *XML API*, and *SOAP API*. This should provide an understanding of how their popularities have changed over time.

Developers using popular languages and frameworks can very likely parse any valid data format you return to them. You can even interchange data in any of the aforementioned data formats (not including SOAP) quite easily, if you're building a common response

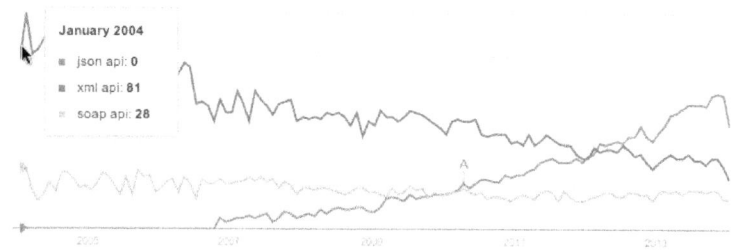

Figure 3.1: Google Trends for JSON API, XML API, and SOAP API

object and swapping serializers. It is crucial that when supporting multiple return formats you adhere to the `Accept` header provided by the Consumer.

Some API architects recommend adding a .json, .xml, or .html file extension to the URL (appended to the Endpoint) for specifying the Content Type to be returned. Unfortunately, with the different extensions added, we've now got different URLs representing the same Resources.

Use the `Accept` header, which is built into the HTTP spec specifically for this purpose, and if you can't provide data in a format the Consumer requests, reply with a `406 Not Acceptable` status.

3.3 Expected Body Content

When a Consumer makes a request to the Server, something needs to be returned as a response. Depending on the HTTP Method and Endpoint being requested, the expected response will differ.

3.3.0.1 GET /{collection}

When performing a GET request to an entire Collection, the Consumer typically expects an array of Resources to be returned. In the simplest form of HTTP APIs, this consists of a single JSON array containing a homogeneous list of resources.

```
[
  {
    "id": "1",
```

3.3. EXPECTED BODY CONTENT

```
    "name": "John Smith",
    "created": "2014-01-01T12:00:00Z",
    "modified": null
  },
  {
    "id": "2",
    "name": "Jane Doe",
    "created": "2014-01-01T12:01:00Z",
    "modified": null
  }
]
```

3.3.0.2 GET /{collection}/{resource_id}

When performing a GET request for a specific resource, the Consumer is expecting to receive the resource object. In a simple HTTP API, this is just the resource as a top level JSON object.

```
{
  "id": "2",
  "name": "Jane Doe",
  "created": "2014-01-01T12:01:00Z",
  "modified": null
}
```

3.3.0.3 POST /{collection}

When performing a POST request to a Collection, the Consumer expects the resource it just created to be returned. In the ideal HTTP API, the object being provided is exactly the same as the object being returned. However, there is very important information being returned to the Consumer which it doesn't already know, such as the `resource_id` and other calculated attributes such as timestamps.

```
{
  "id": "3",
  "name": "Alice Roberts",
  "created": "2014-01-01T12:02:00Z",
  "modified": null
}
```

3.3.0.4 PUT /{collection}/{resource_id}

The result of a PUT operation is the entirety of the resource that was updated, as the root JSON object.

```
{
  "id": "3",
  "name": "Alice Smith",
  "created": "2014-01-01T12:01:00Z",
  "modified": "2014-01-01T12:03:00Z"
}
```

3.3.0.5 PATCH /{collection}/{resource_id}

The result of a PATCH request is exactly the same as the result of a PUT operation. Even though the Consumer may have only acted on some of the attributes, the entire resource is returned.

```
{
  "id": "3",
  "name": "Alicia Smith",
  "created": "2014-01-01T12:01:00Z",
  "modified": "2014-01-01T12:04:00Z"
}
```

3.3.0.6 DELETE /{collection}/{resource_id}

This is the easiest of the bodies to deal with. Once a resource is deleted, you simply return an empty document. No need to return information about the deleted resource. Since no body is present, omit the `Content-Type` header.

3.4 JSON Attribute Conventions

JSON, which stands for *JavaScript Object Notation*, is a subset of JavaScript, and was defined for the purpose of building a language-agnostic data interchange format. It fills mostly the same role that XML was designed to fill, except that it has the side effect of being much more compact, easily deserializing into native objects in most languages, and supporting many different data types (XML technically only supports strings).

That said, there is still quite a bit of freedom that a developer has when representing data using JSON. This section of the book is designed to give you advice for representing data.

3.4.1 Consistency between Resources

Whenever you represent different Resources within the same Collection, each attribute should remain of the same data type. For example, if one Resource has a `name` attribute which is a String, you shouldn't in a different Resource represent it as an Integer.

There are some exceptions, such as when a value doesn't exist, it can be represented as a `null`. In general, keeping the attributes of the same data type will make your API easier for consumers to use, especially those using statically typed languages (*JavaScript* and *PHP* are more forgiving in this regard than a language like *C*).

3.4.2 Booleans

It may be tempting to name your Booleans with a prefix or postfix to symbolize the purpose of the attribute. Common examples of this would be to prefix the variable with `is_` or end it with `_flag`.

This really isn't necessary as attribute names are often self-documenting. For example, if there is an attribute on your User resource called `administrator`, it should be obvious that using a non-Boolean isn't intended.

Another tip with Booleans is that they should usually be a *positive* or *happy* word, as opposed to their negative counterparts. This will prevent developers from having to figure out a double-negative. For example, use `enabled` instead of `disabled`, `public` instead of `private`, and even `keep` instead of `purge`.

3.4.3 Timestamps

There are a multitude of standards for representing dates and times.

3.4.3.1 ISO 8601

The ideal standard for representing dates is the **ISO 8601** [6] standard, and it looks a bit like this:

```
"2014-01-10T03:06:17.396Z"
"2014-01-09T22:06:17+05:00"
```

This format is human readable, lacks redundant information, has variable precision (the microseconds on the end is optional), conveys timezone information (the `Z` means UTC, but an offset can be provided), and is the most popular of standardized date formats.

3.4.3.2 JavaScript Default

JSON is a subset of JavaScript, and JavaScript does have a default format for parsing dates. To see this format generated, create a new `Date` object and convert it to a String. The format of these dates looks a little something like this:

```
"Thu Jan 09 2014 22:06:17 GMT-0500 (EST)"
```

Unfortunately this format is a verbose eyesore. Who cares what day of the week it was?

3.4.3.3 UNIX Epoch

If you wanted something much more terse, you could represent the date as the number of seconds since the Unix Epoch, and it can be stored as an integer:

```
1389323177396
```

This format is a bit too terse. As a human looking at it, you have no idea what date and time it represents! Linux and Unix machines and open source languages can parse that format very easily, however developers using *Microsoft* technology will likely be clueless.

3.4.3.4 SQL Timestamp

Here is another common date format. This is what happens when a developer takes a `TIMESTAMP` directly from a SQL database and outputs it into the response:

```
"2014-01-10 03:06:17"
```

The problem with this format is that it does not convey what timezone the date is in! You may be tempted to use this format, and document the timezone of the server (which we refer to as being *out of band*). However, developers will not remember it, and users of their application will wonder why a newly uploaded image has a modified time of five hours and three seconds ago.

3.4. JSON ATTRIBUTE CONVENTIONS

3.4.4 Resource Identifiers (IDs)

Whenever communicating IDs, transfer them as a String (even if they are numeric). Everything a Consumer does with an ID is in string form anyway. If they make a request to the Resource, the ID is concatenated with another String and used as a URL. If the ID is logged, it is written as a String on disk. And unless the Consumer is doing some shady scraping of the API, the ID should never need to have arithmetic performed with it.

Also, if IDs are always sent as a String, deciding to change from a numeric representation to a different format such as a UUID (e.g. 7d531700-79a5-11e3-979a-a79bcbe406e9) or a Base62 encoded value (e.g. oHg5SJYRHA0) will result in no code changes on the Consumers end.

3.4.5 Nulls

If most Resources have a particular attribute available, and some do not, you should always provide the attribute in the document with a null value, instead of outright removing the attribute.

This will make things easier for Consumers who won't need to check if a JSON attribute exists before attempting to read it.

3.4.6 Arrays

When representing Resources with attributes which represent an array, you should give the attribute a plural name. This signifies to the developer they should expect more than one value.

When an Array shouldn't have any entries, you should typically return an array with nothing in it, instead of returning a null.

3.4.7 Whitespace

Whitespace, while convenient for a human to read, isn't very beneficial to a Consumer, and incurs some extra networking overhead. It's really up to you to decide if you want to add whitespace to the output.

JSON allows for any number of whitespace between keys and values, but if you are going to add whitespace, use a simple and consistent standard. Two spaces for indentation and a single newline is common practice.

3.5 Error Reporting

Errors are an inevitability of any inter-party communication. Users will fat finger an email address, developers will not read the tiny disclaimer you hid in your API documentation, and a database server will occasionally burst into flame. When this happens, the server will of course return a **4XX** or **5XX** HTTP Status Code, but the document body itself should have useful information included.

When designing an error object, there isn't a specific standard that you need to follow. The examples that follow aren't an existing standard, however feel free to use them as a starting point when designing your own errors. Make sure that there is consistency between errors regardless of endpoint.

There are essentially two classes of errors you can account for. The first one is a simple error, where it is easy to point to a specific attribute as being the problem. Let's refer to these as validation errors. The second class of errors are a bit more complex, and may not be easily interpreted by an API Consumer. Let's call these generic errors.

3.5.1 Validation Errors

When an error happens regarding a malformed attribute, provide the Consumer with a reference to the attribute causing the error, as well as a message about what is wrong. Assuming the Consumer is providing a UI for a User to input data, they can display the message for the user to read as well as provide context for the User.

Erroneous Request

```
PUT /v1/users/1

{
  "name": "Rupert Styx",
  "age": "Twenty Eight"
}
```

Error Response

```
400 Bad Request

{
  "error_human": "Inputs not formatted as expected",
```

```
  "error_code": "invalid_attributes",
  "fields": [
    {
      "field": "age",
      "error_human":"Age must be a number between 1 and 100",
      "error_code": "integer_validation"
    }
  ]
}
```

3.5.2 Generic Errors

When an error occurs which can't be traced back to a single input attribute being incorrect, you'll want to return a more generic error construct.

Request

```
POST /v1/animals

{
  "name": "Mittens",
  "type": "kitten"
}
```

Error Response

```
503 Service Unavailable

{
  "error_human": "The Database is currently unavailable.",
  "error_code": "database_unavailable"
}
```

3.5.3 Always Handle Server Errors

Make sure that you catch all errors your server is capable of producing, and *always* return content to the Consumer in the format they are expecting!

This sounds obvious, but it can actually be a lot harder than you think. In PHP, for example, extra care has to be made to catch all errors. By default, PHP and many other web languages/frameworks will return HTML formatted errors.

Consumers will throw all sorts of broken data your way. Experiment with your Server and see what sort of errors you can cause it to produce. Try sending malformed JSON, upload a 100GB file, corrupt the HTTP headers, make 100k concurrent requests, even try removing the underlying code or breaking file permissions and see how your web server handles it.

3.5.4 String-Based Error Codes

In my opinion, there are two types of strings in programming. The first type of string contains human readable text, which includes punctuation and different letter cases and even Unicode symbols. These strings should never be used for comparison. When I program in a language which supports both single and double-quotes for strings, I'll surround these in double quotes.

The other types of strings are computer readable strings. These are much simpler, often used for attributes (you wouldn't use `First Name` as a JSON key, would you?!), and should be all lowercase and contain underscores (or, camelCase, if you're one of *those* people). These strings could pass as names of variables in most languages. I'll usually surround these strings in single quotes.

Returning to the topic of error codes, it is important to provide the Consumer with *both* a computer readable error code, as well as a human readable error message. The code can be looked up and have logic applied to it by the Consumer. The human readable message can change at any point if a translation changes or any type of rewrite happens.

Many APIs I've seen include the use of numeric error codes. For example, if there was an error with a database transaction being committed, the error code might be `2091`. A third-party developer working with the API and coming across that error is going to have absolutely no idea what that number means, and will have to go look it up in the API docs. If that message were instead `database_transaction_failure`, the developer is going to have somewhat of a clue as to what just happened and will be able to compensate faster.

The Stripe API [7, #Errors] makes great use of error strings for conveying error codes. One such example is `expired_card`, which as a third-party developer, you immediately know that the user-supplied card has expired.

3.6 Responses should Mimic Requests

As a general rule, a Response resource structure should closely resemble the equivalent Request resource. This means that the same attribute names and values are used for Requests as well as Responses.

There are of course a few exceptions. A PATCH, for example, only affects a partial document. A POST won't have certain server-calculated attributes (like an ID or a created timestamp). PATCH and PUTs won't have certain read-only attributes (e.g. created and modified times). These differences in attributes should be minimal when possible.

Whenever dealing with the values of attributes, they should always be the same format. A good philosophy to follow is that request objects should be a strict subset of response objects.

3.6.1 Acceptable Discrepancy

In this example, the differences between the Request and the Response documents are minimal. Some of the values are read-only, and calculated on the server (e.g. `id`, `modified`, and `created`). Some of the attributes have default values (e.g. `enabled`), which is fine too, as long as these are documented.

Request

```
POST /users

{
  "role": "administrator",
  "name": "Rupert Styx"
}
```

Response

```
{
  "id": "12",
  "role": "administrator",
  "created": "2014-01-15T02:40:46.049Z",
  "modified": null,
  "name": "Rupert Styx",
  "enabled": true
}
```

3.6.2 Avoidable Discrepancy

In this example, during a POST to the `users` endpoint, there is a `role` attribute, which is a string containing possible user roles, such as `administrator` or `moderator`. However, in the response, that same data becomes a Boolean of whether or not the user is an administrator. This increases the amount of attribute names the Consumer needs to keep track of.

Request

```
POST /users

{
  "role": "administrator",
  "name": "Rupert Styx"
}
```

Response

```
{
  "id": "12",
  "administrator": true,
  "name": "Rupert Styx"
}
```

Chapter 4

The API Ecosystem

4.1 API Versioning

No matter what you are building and how much planning you do beforehand, your core application will change, your company will pivot, your data relationships will alter, and attributes will be added and removed from resources. This is just how software development works, and is especially true if your project is alive and used by many people.

Remember than an API is a published contract between a Server and a Consumer. If you make changes to the API and these changes break backwards compatibility, you will break deployed applications and third party developers will resent you for it. Do it enough, and they may migrate to somebody else's service. To ensure your application continually evolves *and* you keep developers happy, you need to occasionally introduce new versions of the API while still allowing old versions to function.

Facebook is notorious for making backwards-breaking changes to their API. Indeed, while researching their Graph API, I could not find any mention of a scheme for performing versioning.

> As a side note, if you are simply *adding* new features to your API, such as new attributes to a resource (assuming they are not required to be set), or if you are *adding* new Endpoints, you do not need to increment your API version number as these changes do not break backwards compatibility. You will want to update your API Documentation, of course.

Over time you can deprecate old versions of the API. To deprecate a feature doesn't mean to shut if off or diminish quality, but to alert developers that the older version will be removed on a specific date and that they should upgrade to a newer version.

4.1.1 Requesting a Specific Version

There are three common methods HTTP APIs use for communicating which version of the API to use.

4.1.1.1 Versioning via a URL Segment

The method which is the easiest for most Consumers to handle to to add a URL segment after the root location of the API and the specific Endpoints. Changing the URL is the easiest thing a developer can do.

The most common argument against this approach is that /v1/users and /v2/users supposedly represent the same data, and using redundant URLs for the same data violates good HTTP design principles. However, the two URLs likely *do not* represent the same data, as one could be abstracting data completely different than the other. There's also no guarantee endpoints will be named the same between versions.

```
https://api.example.org/v1/*
```

It is customary to use the letter **v** followed by an integer when versioning this way. Due to the nature of APIs, changing versions often is discouraged, and point releases usually aren't needed.

LinkedIn, and Google+ use a v and an integer (e.g. /v3/). Dropbox just uses an integer (e.g. /1/). Twitter uses a v and a decimal (e.g. /v1.1/). NetFlix uses a ?v= and a decimal URL parameter (not an Endpoint URL segment, but still part of the URL).

4.1.1.2 Versioning via the Accept Header

Another method is to use a custom Accept header, where the Consumer specifies the type of content they are expecting along with the version of the API. This method may be the *purest* as far as API design is concerned.

The Accept header offers a way to specify generic and less generic content types, as well as specifying fall-backs. In the example below, we are requesting a more specific version of JSON, conceptually, Version 1 of the API JSON.

`Accept: application/json+v1`

GitHub uses an Accept header formatted `application/vnd.github.v3+json` to interact with a specific version of their API. If omitted, the Consumer interacts with the *beta* version.

4.1.1.3 Versioning via a Custom Header

Another method is to use a custom header. This is quite similar to the previous method. Consumers would still use the normal Accept header they've been using.

`X-Api-Version: 1`

Joyent CloudAPI and Copy.com APIs use this header.

4.2 Authentication and Authorization

There are two common paradigms in which your API may authorize Consumers. Using the Two-Legged paradigm, there are two parties involved; a Consumer and your Server. In the Three-Legged paradigm, there are three parties involved, a Consumer, your Server, and a User who has (or will have) an account with both services.

In theory, your API could use both methods of authorization for different areas. Also, there may be some sections of the API which can be accessed anonymously and can entirely bypass the authorization process.

4.2.1 Two-Legged Authentication (2LA)

As you can tell in Figure 4.1, the concept of Two-Legged Authentication (*2LA*) is quite simple. Essentially, the Consumer needs a way to authenticate themselves with the API. Due to the stateless nature of HTTP, this authentication needs to be present with every request.

Modern websites make use of sessions for handling this state, where a session identifier is passed along with every request via

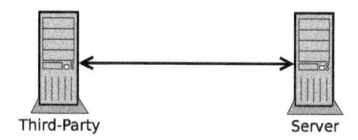

Figure 4.1: Two-Legged Authentication (2LA)

cookie. With an API, you would never require the use of a cookie (they're typically difficult to work with programmatically), but the method we will use is conceptually similar.

> The introduction of site-wide state information in the form of HTTP cookies is an example of an inappropriate extension to the protocol. Cookie interaction fails to match REST's application state model, often resulting in confusion for the typical browser application.[8, Page 145]

The HTTP protocol gives us a header called `Authorization` for passing around this sort of information. While there are many different ways to do API authorization, many of them make use of this header in some manner.

4.2.1.1 Basic HTTP Authentication

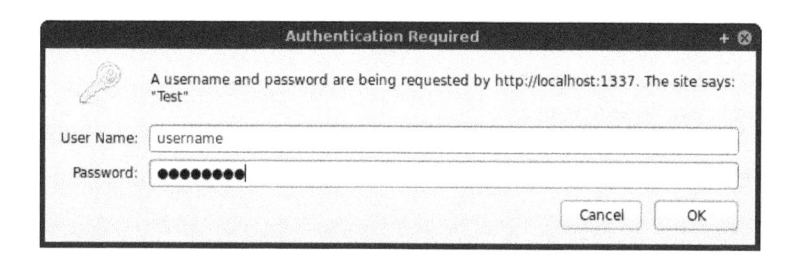

Figure 4.2: Basic HTTP Authentication Dialog in FireFox

The *classical* method of performing authentication is called Basic HTTP Auth [9], where a User Agent (meaning a web browser or Consumer) first makes a GET request to a protected resource. The Server responds with the `401 Unauthorized` header, and the User Agent displays a dialog prompting the user for a username and password.

4.2. AUTHENTICATION AND AUTHORIZATION

First Request

```
GET /protected HTTP/1.1
Host: www.example.org
Accept: text/html
```

Unauthorized Response

```
HTTP/1.1 401 Unauthorized
Date: Thu, 9 Jan 2014 23:35:00 GMT
WWW-Authenticate: Basic realm="Example"
```

At this point, the user either clicks cancel and is taken to an error screen and chooses to go somewhere else, or they enter correct credentials and click Authorize. Entering the wrong credentials typically results in the Server sending back the same Unauthorized status.

The credentials supplied by the user are transmitted as follows: The username (which cannot contain :) is concatenated with :, and then concatenated with the password. This text is then Base64 Encoded and sent in the Authorization header. As you can probably guess, this is extremely insecure if done over unencrypted HTTP.

Authorized Request

```
GET /protected HTTP/1.1
Host: www.example.org
Accept: text/html
Authorization: Basic QWxhZGRpbjpvcGVuIHNlc2FtZQ==
```

Finally, the Server provides the User Agent with the protected content which the user has requested. This exact same Authorization header is sent with every subsequent request.

Implementing HTTP Basic Authorization to your API is just as easy, except that instead of having a browser on the other end, it would be a Consumer of your API. The initial unauthorized request wouldn't need to be performed as the Consumer would know ahead of time that it needs to first be authorized. If the Consumer does provide incorrect credentials, the server would still reply with a `401 Unauthorized` status.

4.2.1.2 Alternatives to Basic Auth

You can always invent your own method of auth where you supply the Consumer with a single randomly-generated and impossible-to-guess token, which they simply provide in the Authorization header (this concept is often referred to as an *Auth Token*). Third parties may want the ability to revoke Auth Tokens, and to generate multiple ones for their Application. Make sure that you provide an administration interface so developers can provision and revoke these tokens themselves.

4.2.2 Three-Legged Authentication (3LA)

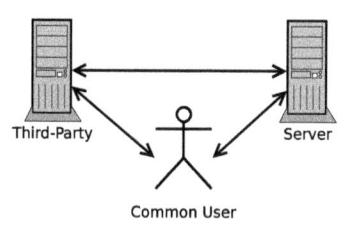

Figure 4.3: Three-Legged Authentication (3LA)

As you can see in Figure 4.3, Three-Legged Authentication (*3LA*) is a bit more complex. Instead of passing messages between two parties (one channel), messages need to be communicated between three parties (three channels). A user likely trusts your application with their username and password, however they don't trust a third-party Consumer. The user would also like the ability to revoke the third-parties access to their data, without the need to change their username and password.

The complexities of *3LA* are far too intricate to exemplify in this book, so you'll want to read more information from a different source. At a high level, they provide a method for a Consumer to sign requests and to validate they are who they say they are. *3LA* also provides a method for users to grant privileges so Consumers can access specific data. Users can revoke permissions from Consumers at any point. Of course, the Server can also revoke a Consumers privileges.

OAuth 2.0 [10] is the De-Facto standard for performing *3LA* in modern HTTP APIs. With each Request, the Server can be sure it knows which Consumer is making a request, which User

4.2. AUTHENTICATION AND AUTHORIZATION

they are making requests on behalf of, and provide a standardized method for expiring access or allowing users to revoke access from a Consumer, all without the need for a third-party Consumer to know the users login credentials.

There is also the older OAuth 1.0a [11] standard, which solves mostly the same problems. This standard works by requiring a hash of OAuth attributes sent over the wire, which includes concepts such as a timestamp and a nonce. These are common in cryptographic systems for providing security, such as preventing replay attacks, and are mostly made irrelevant by sending data over HTTPS. Whichever method you ultimately choose, ensure it is trustworthy and well-documented and has many different libraries available for the languages and platforms which your Consumers will likely be using.

> OAuth 1.0a, while it is technically the most secure of the options, can be quite difficult to implement. While maintaining an OAuth 1.0a provider, I was surprised by the number of developers who had to implement their own library since one didn't already exist for their language. After spending many hours debugging cryptic *invalid signature* errors, I really must suggest choosing OAuth 2.0.

4.2.3 Real-World Usage

Choosing which authentication mechanism to use for your service may be made easier by looking at what other services use, and the reasoning by choosing each method.

- **Twitter**: OAuth 1.0a, xAuth (proprietary), OAuth 2.0
    - OAuth 1.0a is kept around to support legacy Consumers
    - xAuth was created to bring some OAuth 2.0 features to OAuth 1.0a (e.g. desktop login)
- **GitHub**: OAuth 2.0, Basic Auth
    - Basic Auth will leak user credentials to third-parties
    - Basic Auth likely chosen for developers testing their own apps
    - Github users *are* developers after all

- **Mailgun**: Basic Auth
  - Mailgun is purely *2LA*, so Basic Auth is a fine choice
  - Using Basic Auth makes it easier for novice developers to test the API
- **Facebook Graph**: OAuth 2.0
  - The userbase is Facebooks greatest asset, and is definitely a *3LA* service
  - Facebook is a big target for hackers
- **Dropbox**: OAuth 1.0a, OAuth 2.0
  - OAuth 1.0a is for supporting legacy Consumers
  - OAuth 2.0 is the preferred method for authenticating with Dropbox

4.3 Consumer Permissions

Permissions are a way of specifying which Consumers have access to what data, and more specifically, how they are allowed to manipulate this data.

When dealing with *2LA*, the process for deciding Permissions is likely to be handled very simply. For example, if your Service is owned by *Widgets, Inc.*, and this company trusts *Gadgets, Co.* with certain features of the API, *Widgets, Inc.* will probably manually assign *Gadgets, Co.* with more liberal permissions. However, Company *Hackers, LLC*, which is otherwise unknown to *Widgets, Inc.*, will get the default restrictive permissions. Or, perhaps additional permissions can be earned by paying a fee or mailing in a photo ID.

Regarding *3LA*, the Consumer needs to have the ability to specify which resources belonging to the user they would like to interact with. When the user authorizes the Consumer, the user is usually prompted with a GUI to review permissions, perhaps make a decision or two, and either allow or deny access. You've very likely seen these permission prompts with services like Twitter (seen in Figure 4.4), Facebook, LinkedIn, etc.

Some services will allow a User to disable permissions (older versions of Facebook allowed this), other services will require the permissions to be accepted or denied outright. You can choose

Figure 4.4: Twitter OAuth Permissions

whichever approach you'd like with your service. Do keep in mind that Consumers which don't anticipate the permissions changing could break in weird ways.

4.3.1 Per-Authorization Permissions

The method for specifying permissions will vary depending on the authorization mechanism your API implements. With OAuth 1.0a a standard didn't exist as part of the spec. The Server can accept an additional parameter called scope (or whatever you choose) during the Request Token generation phase. This parameter could be a JSON object representing the permissions the Consumer is requesting. By passing this parameter during the authorization step, a Consumer is able to get per-user permissions.

The following permissions object could represent a common social media website. It represents a Consumer which wishes to get information about a users profile as well as make changes to their profile, send the user emails using the service (although not have access to their email address), as well as retrieve a list of friends, add new friends, and remove existing friends.

```
{
  "profile": [ "read", "write" ],
  "email": [ "send" ],
  "friends": [ "read", "add", "remove" ]
}
```

When the user authenticates the Consumer, they would see a list of each of the permissions the Consumer is asking for. Some of them which grant destructive or powerful capabilities such as adding and removing friends or changing the users profile should be highlighted for emphasis.

Here's an example taken from Coinbase [12]. They adhere to the OAuth 2.0 spec for sending permissions by using a simple list of keywords representing permissions separated by spaces (which are encoded as + symbols). This request would allow the consumer to `buy`, `sell`, `send`, and `request` Bitcoins on behalf of the authenticated user.

```
https://coinbase.com/oauth/authorize?response_type=code
    &client_id=YOUR_CLIENT_ID&redirect_uri=YOUR_CALLBACK_URL
    &scope=buy+sell+send+request
```

4.3.2 Default Consumer Permissions

When a Consumer registers their application with your Server, assuming permissions will need to be the same for every user of their application, they can specify the permissions all at once. This would probably be done from a UI, such as providing a list of checkboxes where each checkbox represents a permission. Figure 4.5 is an example of Per-Consumer permissions used by Copy.com.

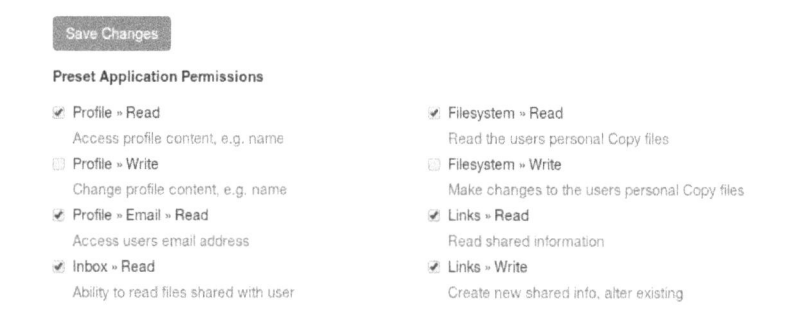

Figure 4.5: Copy.com Default Consumer Permissions

Ideally, your Server could even allow for both of these mechanisms to work in parallel (accepting preset permissions, to be overwritten by optional per-user permissions). This gives developers the greatest amount of control and convenience.

4.4 Rate Limiting

Rate limiting is a feature which can be implemented in an API to prevent Consumers from making diminishing Server stability by making too many requests. Consumers can be given a limit on the number of requests they make. This limit could be per-Consumer, per-User-per-Consumer, or whatever you decide. If limits are per-Consumer, depending on how much your Server trusts the Consumer, the limits could be higher. Some services even offer a subscription fee for increasing this limit.

If your API makes use of rate limits, be sure information about the limit can be accesses programmatically. The following is an example of how GitHub conveys rate limit information to third parties with the introduction of `X-RateLimit` headers. The `-Limit` header represents the total limit per period of time, `-Remaining` is how many requests remain to be made during this period of time, and `-Reset` is a timestamp for when the period resets.

```
HTTP/1.1 403 Forbidden
Date: Tue, 20 Aug 2013 14:50:41 GMT
Status: 403 Forbidden
X-RateLimit-Limit: 60
X-RateLimit-Remaining: 0
X-RateLimit-Reset: 1377013266

{
    "message": "API rate limit exceeded. \
        See http://developer.github.com/v3/ \
        #rate-limiting for details."
}
```

4.5 API Analytics

Keep track of the version/endpoints being used by Consumers of your API. This can be as simple as incrementing an integer in a database each time a request is made. There are many reasons that keeping track of API Analytics is beneficial such as optimizing the most commonly requested Endpoints to reduce Server load.

When you do deprecate a version of your API, you can actually contact third-party developers using deprecated features. This is a convenient approach for reminding developers to upgrade before killing off the old version.

If you can, try to keep track of a matrix worth of analytics data. For example, which endpoint is used, in which version of the API, and by which Consumer (and perhaps even which *3LA User*). If you get angry users telling you that certain features are broken, having this information will be very helpful for diagnosing problems.

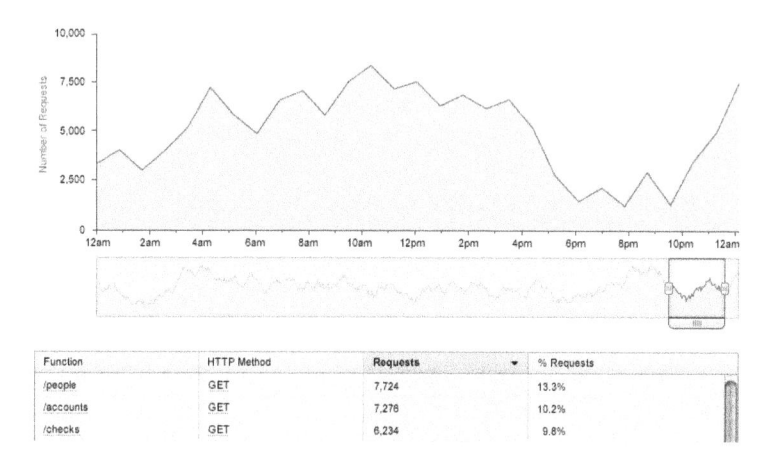

Figure 4.6: Screenshot of Apigee Analytics

Figure 4.6 is an example of the sort of API Analytics captured by the company Apigee.

4.6 Documentation

Writing documentation is vital to the success of an API. If consumers don't know how to use an API, they won't use it.

Make your Documentation available to the public, and especially search engines. Keeping documentation hidden behind a login prompt will have a few detriments. Developers won't be able to find documentation using a search engine, developers will be annoyed when they have to login and re-navigate to the docs, and potential developers won't know the capabilities of your API before deciding if they should sign up.

Avoid using automatic documentation generators! If you do use them, at least make sure you're cleaning up the output and making it presentable. Generated docs can be useful with libraries where code connects directly to it, or even Remote Procedure Call (RPC) style APIs where the code and API are closely connected.

However, automatically-generated documentation can often leave much to be desired regarding quality and navigability.

Do not truncate example Resource request and response bodies, just show the whole thing (Collections can be truncated to only a few Resources, of course). Even specify which HTTP headers the Consumer should expect to see. Make use of a syntax highlighter in your documentation as color-highlighted JSON is much easier to parse with human eyes.

Document expected response codes and possible error messages for each endpoint, and what could have gone wrong to cause those errors to happen. Dedicate a place where anticipated error codes can be looked up as well.

Make sure your documentation can be printed. CSS is a powerful thing; don't be afraid to hide that sidebar when the docs are printed. Even if nobody prints a physical copy, you'd be surprised at how many developers like to print to PDF for offline perusing.

Documentation can either be split into many different webpages, or kept on one long page. If you are keeping documentation on one long page, break it up into sections with anchor tags and provide a Table of Contents so that developers can link to parts and share links with others. Long documentation can be hard to browse, and search engine results won't always link to the proper section of the document (this issue plagues the Backbone.js documentation).

4.7 Convenience of Developer Testing

Providing convenient tools will allow developers to quickly test API commands without having to paste sample code into their own application. This allows them to get familiar with your API much quicker.

4.7.1 Web-Based Developer Console

A Web-based developer console, e.g. Figure 4.7, will allow developers to test API commands without ever leaving the documentation website.

You will already need a website where third-party developers can register their applications, get authentication credentials, read documentation, etc. This is a great place to put an API Console.

Ensure the Developer Console is easy and efficient. Perhaps even provide them with a default user account which resets every

```
PUT http://api.example.com/v1/user/1
```

Method   API Endpoint   Send Request
PUT   ▼   user/1   Submit

HTTP Request Body (POST/PUT/PATCH Requests)
```
{
  "first_name": "Thomas",
  "last_name": "Hunter II"
}
```

Figure 4.7: Example API Console

hour using a CRON job. Maybe by clicking a single button their application listing, the *3LA* credentials are automatically applied and the developer can begin making API calls on behalf of their application immediately.

If possible use URL parameters for the Developer Console form when it submits. This way, from within the documentation, a developer could click a link describing an API Endpoint and immediately be taken to the console where the Endpoint is executed.

4.7.2 Providing cURL Commands

cURL is a command-line utility available for many platforms (it even comes shipped with many Linux distributions). You very likely have installed cURL as a dependency for another project which makes HTTP requests.

Services such as Mailgun, Stripe, and even GitHub provide sample cURL commands. When doing *2LA*, sample queries are very easy to execute (3LA is often more difficult due to the required steps beforehand).

While cURL is available for *Windows*, if your service is primarily consumed by developers using *Microsoft* technologies, providing example cURL commands may not be as beneficial as many of these developers would not have cURL or find it as beneficial.

4.7.2.1 Example cURL Command

This is the example cURL command displayed on the Mailgun homepage [13]. The provided API key is even functional, so by pasting this command into a terminal, a developer can instantly make a real API call!

4.7. CONVENIENCE OF DEVELOPER TESTING

```
curl -s --user 'api:key-3ax6xnjp29jd6fds4gc373sgvjxteol0' \
  https://api.mailgun.net/v2/samples.mailgun.org/messages \
  -F from='Excited User <excited@samples.mailgun.org>' \
  -F to='devs@mailgun.net' \
  -F subject='Hello' \
  -F text='Testing some Mailgun awesomeness!'
```

Chapter 5

HTTP API Standards

5.1 Hypermedia API's

It would be irresponsible to cover HTTP-based API design without mentioning Hypermedia/REST (Representational State Transfer) [14]. Hypermedia APIs may very-well be the future of HTTP API design. It really is an amazing concept, going *back to the roots* of how HTTP (and HTML) was intended to work.

With the examples we've been covering until this point, the URL Endpoints are part of the contract between the API and the Consumer. These Endpoints must be known by the Consumer ahead of time, and changing them means the Consumer is no longer able to communicate with the API.

API Consumers are far from being the only user agent making HTTP requests on the Internet. Humans with their web browsers are the most common user agent making HTTP requests. Humans of course are *not* locked into this predefined Endpoint URL contract that most HTTP APIs are.

What makes us humans so special? We're able to read content, click links for headings which look interesting, and in general explore a website and interpret content to get where we want to go. If a URL changes, we're not affected (unless we bookmarked a page, in which case we go to the homepage and find a new route to our beloved article).

The Hypermedia API concept works the same way a human would. Requesting the Root of the API returns a listing of URLs which point perhaps to each collection of information, and describing each collection in a way which the Consumer can understand.

Providing IDs for each resource isn't important as long as a URL to the resource is provided.

With the Consumer of a Hypermedia API crawling links and gathering information, URLs are always up-to-date within responses and do not need to be known as part of a contract. If a URL is ever cached, and a subsequent request returns a 404, the Consumer can simply go back to the root and discover the content again.

When retrieving a list of Resources within a Collection, an attribute containing a complete URL for the individual Resources are returned. When performing a POST/PATCH/PUT, the response could be a **3XX** redirect to the complete resource.

JSON doesn't quite give us the semantics we need for specifying which attributes are URLs, nor how URLs relate to the current document (although, as we'll soon see, there are some standards for doing this). HTML, as you should already know, does provide this information! We may very well see our APIs come full circle and return to consuming HTML. Considering how far we've come with CSS, one day it may be common practice for APIs and Websites to use the exact same URLs and HTML content.

Imagine a tool on the internet that you want to use. It could be Google Calendar, or Meetup, or Facebook Events. Also imagine that you want to use other tools too, like email or instant messengers. Normally, integrations between tools are only convenient if you're using a massive suite of tools, such as what is offered by Microsoft or Google. As an example, Google Mail integrates very tightly with Google Calendar and Google+ to provide a seamless user experience.

Now, imagine that these disparate tools by different companies can work with each other as tightly as these massive suites of tools. Often times when a company builds a single product it is better than the equivalent component of a larger suite. This combination of specific, well-built tools working seamlessly with other services becomes the best of both worlds! The process could theoretically work automatically, with the different services discovering each other and configuring themselves to play nicely. This is a future offered by hypermedia-based APIs.

5.1.1 ATOM: An Early Hypermedia API

ATOM [15], a distant cousin of RSS, is likely one of the first mainstream Hypermedia APIs (except for HTML itself). ATOM is valid XML, and therefore easy to parse. Links to other documents use

5.2. RESPONSE DOCUMENT STANDARDS

a `link` tag, and specify both the URL (using the `href` attribute), as well as the documents relation to the current document (using the `rel` attribute).

```xml
<?xml version="1.0" encoding="utf-8"?>
<feed xmlns="http://www.w3.org/2005/Atom">
  <title>Example Feed</title>
  <subtitle>A subtitle.</subtitle>
  <link href="http://example.org/feed/" rel="self" />
  <link href="http://example.org/" />
  <id>urn:uuid:60a76c80-d399-11d9-b91C-0003939e0af6</id>
  <updated>2003-12-13T18:30:02Z</updated>
  <entry>
    <title>Atom-Powered Robots Run Amok</title>
    <link href="http://example.org/2003/12/13/atom03" />
    <link rel="alternate" type="text/html"
        href="http://example.org/2003/12/13/atom03.html"/>
    <link rel="edit"
        href="http://example.org/2003/12/13/atom03/edit"/>
    <id>urn:uuid:1225c695-cfb8-4ebb-aaaa-80da344efa6a</id>
    <updated>2003-12-13T18:30:02Z</updated>
    <summary>Some text.</summary>
      <author>
        <name>John Doe</name>
        <email>johndoe@example.com</email>
      </author>
  </entry>
</feed>
```

5.2 Response Document Standards

When responding with a document representing, say, a Collection, it is usually adequate to return a top-level array containing each resource object. Likewise, when responding with a document representing a resource, simply returning a top-level object containing the resource is usually good-enough.

However, there are some standards which forward-thinking API Architects have developed for encapsulating these objects in a standardized envelope. These envelopes give the Consumer context when parsing the responses.

For example, if making a filtered request limits a Collection response to contain only 10 Resources, how do you let the Consumer know how many total records exist? How do you convey expected data types programmatically? These different response document standards provide methods for returning this meta data.

5.2.1 JSON Schema

JSON Schema [16] provides a method for describing the attributes provided by a API endpoints. This description is written in JSON in such a way as to be both human-readable and easy to work with programmatically. Using JSON Schema, a Consumer could easily automate data validation and generation of CRUD forms.

5.2.1.1 Example JSON Schema Document

```
{
  "title": "Example Schema",
  "type": "object",
  "properties": {
    "firstName": {
      "type": "string"
    },
    "lastName": {
      "type": "string"
    },
    "age": {
      "description": "Age in years",
      "type": "integer",
      "minimum": 0
    }
  },
  "required": ["firstName", "lastName"]
}
```

5.2.2 JSON API

The JSON API [17] spec provided a standardized format for structuring response documents by introducing some reserved attributes which have special meaning (e.g. `id` must be used for identifying a resource, a convention we've been otherwise following).

An notable feature of JSON API is that is also provides a method for returning not only a requested resource but also other resources which it depends on, as if anticipating the Consumers next request(s).

5.2. RESPONSE DOCUMENT STANDARDS

5.2.2.1 Example JSON API Document

```
{
  "links": {
    "posts.author": {
      "href": "http://example.com/people/{posts.author}",
      "type": "people"
    },
    "posts.comments": {
      "href": "http://example.com/comments/{posts.comments}",
      "type": "comments"
    }
  },
  "posts": [{
    "id": "1",
    "title": "Rails is Omakase",
    "links": {
      "author": "9",
      "comments": [ "1", "2" ]
    }
  }],
  "linked": {
    "people": [{
      "id": "9",
      "name": "@d2h"
    }],
    "comments": [{
      "id": "1",
      "body": "Mmmmmakase"
    }, {
      "id": "2",
      "body": "I prefer unagi"
    }]
  }
}
```

5.2.3 Siren

The Siren Hypermedia [18] spec provides a standard method for representing resources and what actions can be performed on said resources. It is a Hypermedia API so the URL for performing an action or linking to a Resource is provided within the document.

5.2.3.1 Example Siren Document

```
{
```

```
  "class": [ "order" ],
  "properties": {
     "orderNumber": 42,
     "itemCount": 3,
     "status": "pending"
  },
  "entities": [
    {
      "class": [ "items", "collection" ],
      "rel": [ "http://x.io/rels/order-items" ],
      "href": "http://api.x.io/orders/42/items"
    },
    {
      "class": [ "info", "customer" ],
      "rel": [ "http://x.io/rels/customer" ],
      "properties": {
        "customerId": "pj123",
        "name": "Peter Joseph"
      },
      "links": [ {"rel":["self"],
        "href":"http://api.x.io/customers/pj123"} ]
    }
  ],
  "actions": [
    {
      "name": "add-item",
      "title": "Add Item",
      "method": "POST",
      "href": "http://api.x.io/orders/42/items",
      "type": "application/x-www-form-urlencoded",
      "fields": [
        {"name":"orderNumber","type":"hidden","value":"42"},
        { "name": "productCode", "type": "text" },
        { "name": "quantity", "type": "number" }
      ]
    }
  ],
  "links": [
    { "rel": [ "self" ], "href":"http://api.x.io/orders/42"},
    {"rel":["previous"],"href":"http://api.x.io/orders/41"},
    { "rel": [ "next" ],"href": "http://api.x.io/orders/43"}
  ]
}
```

5.3 Alternatives to URL-based API's

Up until now, we've placed a large emphasis on the importance of a URL in our HTTP-based API's. However, there are some standards you should be aware of which have a small emphasis on the URL, typically serving all requests through a single URL.

5.3.1 JSON RPC

JSON RPC [19] is a relatively popular alternative to REST for exposing functionality over a network. Whereas REST is required to be accessed via HTTP, JSON RPC doesn't have a protocol requirement. It can be sent over sockets, be used with Inter Process Communication (IPC), and of course, HTTP.

Unlike REST which requires an abstraction of Server businesslogic and data into simple objects which can be acted upon using CRUD, JSON RPC calls will typically map to existing functions within your application.

When a client makes a call using JSON RPC, they specify the name of a function to execute, as well as arguments to the function. Arguments can be in the form of either ordered parameters (using a JSON Array), or named parameters (using a JSON Object).

The important part of the specification is the envelope which the data adheres to. The concept of a URL doesn't really exist (if you're using JSON RPC over HTTP, there's usually a single URL which all requests are sent through, and each request is likely sent as a POST).

JSON RPC is mostly useful for situations where you don't have an HTTP server, for example multiplayer games or embedded systems or simple communication applications. If you already have an HTTP Server for your product or service, REST is likely a better solution for you.

With HTTP, every Request and Response is guaranteed to be paired together correctly. Due to the asynchronous nature of sockets and other such communication protocols, Requests need to provide a unique ID value, and the corresponding Response needs to provide the same ID.

JSON RPC also has mechanisms for sending batches of operations at once, and in some situations can compliment a RESTful API.

5.3.1.1 Example JSON RPC Request

{"jsonrpc":"2.0","method":"subtract","params":[42,23],"id":1}

5.3.1.2 Example JSON RPC Response

{"jsonrpc": "2.0", "result": 19, "id": 1}

5.3.2 SOAP

Worth mentioning is Simple Object Access Protocol (SOAP) [20], which is a term you've very likely heard of. SOAP is a sort of successor to an older technology called XML RPC. As you've probably guessed, XML RPC is similar to JSON RPC, as both are forms of Remote Procedure Call protocols.

SOAP is useful for describing services exposed over the network, and is transport agnostic just like JSON RPC, although most implementations use it over HTTP. Partly due to the waning popularity of XML in comparison to JSON, SOAP is often looked down upon due to the verbosity and the bulkiness of document sizes.

SOAP is mostly used in larger corporate environments.

5.3.2.1 Example SOAP Request

```
<?xml version="1.0"?>
<soap:Envelope
    xmlns:soap="http://www.w3.org/2003/05/soap-envelope">
  <soap:Header>
  </soap:Header>
  <soap:Body>
    <m:GetStockPrice xmlns:m="http://www.example.org/stock">
      <m:StockName>IBM</m:StockName>
    </m:GetStockPrice>
  </soap:Body>
</soap:Envelope>
```

References

[1] Corey Ballou. Why we chose api first development, 2013.
http://blog.pop.co/post/67465239611/why-we-chose-api-first-development

[2] GitHub, Inc. GitHub v3 API, 2014.
http://developer.github.com/v3

[3] Twitter, Inc. Twitter v1.1 API, 2014.
https://dev.twitter.com/docs/api/1.1

[4] J. Gregorio, R. Fielding, M. Hadley, M. Nottingham, and D. Orchard. RFC 6570: URI Template, 2012.
https://tools.ietf.org/html/rfc6570

[5] R. Fielding, J. Gettys, J. Mogul, H. Frystyk, L. Masinter, P. Leach, and T. Berners-Lee. RFC 2616: Hypertext Transfer Protocol – HTTP/1.1, 1999.
https://tools.ietf.org/html/rfc2616

[6] International Organization for Standardization. ISO 8601: Data elements and interchange formats – Information interchange – Representation of dates and times, 1988.
https://en.wikipedia.org/wiki/Iso8601

[7] Stripe, Inc. Stripe API Reference, 2014.
https://stripe.com/docs/api

[8] Roy T. Fielding and Richard N. Taylor. *ACM Transactions on Internet Technology (TOIT)*, volume 2. ACM, University of California, Irvine, 2002.
http://www.ics.uci.edu/~taylor/documents/2002-REST-TOIT.pdf

[9] J. Franks, P. Hallam-Baker, J. Hostetler, S. Lawrence, P. Leach, A. Luotonen, and L. Stewart. RFC 2617: HTTP Authentication: Basic and Digest Access Authentication, 1999.
https://tools.ietf.org/html/rfc2617

[10] Ed. D. Hardt. RFC 6749: The OAuth 2.0 Authorization Framework, 2012.
https://tools.ietf.org/html/rfc6749

[11] Ed. E. Hammer-Lahav. RFC 5849: The OAuth 1.0 Protocol, 2010.
https://tools.ietf.org/html/rfc5849

[12] Coinbase. API Authentication, 2014.
https://coinbase.com/docs/api/authentication

[13] Mailgun, Inc. Homepage, 2014.
http://www.mailgun.com

[14] Roy T. Fielding. Architectural Styles and the Design of Network-based Software Architectures.
http://www.ics.uci.edu/~fielding/pubs/dissertation/rest_arch_style.htm

[15] Wikipedia. Atom (standard): Example of an Atom 1.0 feed.
https://en.wikipedia.org/wiki/Atom_%28standard%29#Example_of_an_Atom_1.0_feed

[16] JSON Schema. Homepage.
http://json-schema.org

[17] JSON API. Homepage.
http://jsonapi.org

[18] Kevin Swiber. Siren: A Hypermedia Specification for Representing Entities.
http://sirenspec.org

[19] The JSON-RPC Working Group. JSON-RPC 2.0 Specification.
http://www.jsonrpc.org/specification

[20] Wikipedia. SOAP (Simple Object Access Protocol).
https://en.wikipedia.org/wiki/SOAP

Lightning Source UK Ltd.
Milton Keynes UK
UKHW020752200722
406119UK00009B/914